GOD

I'm gonna make you proud of *me*

JACQUELINE THOMAS

Xulon Press
2301 Lucien Way #415
Maitland, FL 32751
407.339.4217
www.xulonpress.com

© 2021 by Jacqueline Thomas

All rights reserved solely by the author. The author guarantees all contents are original and do not infringe upon the legal rights of any other person or work. No part of this book may be reproduced in any form without the permission of the author. The views expressed in this book are not necessarily those of the publisher.

Paperback ISBN-13: 978-1-6628-0339-0

Ebook ISBN-13: 978-1-6628-0340-6

TABLE OF CONTENTS

Don't Pity Me 1

Time Will Tell 3

He Has Always Been There 5

Don't Complain 7

"My God" 9

"A Friend Indeed" 11

"Pray" 13

"Never Alone" 15

Lift My Head Up! 17

My Blessings 19

"Glitter & Gold" 21

"Jesus" 23

"God" 25

"Forgive Me" 27

"Smile" 29

"Keep Striving" 31

God, Come In 33

"It Happened" 35

I Love You 37

"Life" 39

"Time" 41

"Praise" 43

Hell on Earth 45

"Never Let Me Down" 47

"Stop the Violence" 49

Telling Lies 51

Mercy & Grace 53

"Rain" 55

"Let Go" 57

"To Whom I Belong" 59

"Some of Them" 61

"Give Me a Topic" 65

"Fasting" 67

"Change" 69

"Can't Judge Me" 71

"Favor Ain't Fair" 73

"Coronavirus" 75

DON'T PITY ME

04-01-20

Born in this world, I guess my momma was glad I was a girl. I didn't have no hair just one little curl on the top of my head. I'm just repeating what my momma said. I didn't know what life had ahead for me to endure —a lot of trials and tribulations, that one thing's for sure. Growing up as a kid I didn't get much, only my stepfather had a gig. I was a child and I didn't complain, 'cause if I did things still wouldn't change. During this time I learned of a man, and JESUS was His name. I knew then things would be alright. I just had to hold on tight to Him. Little did I know I was hanging on a limb.

    Grew on up to be a young lady; of course, you know my hormones were driving me crazy. Back slid and experimented with weed. I still got down on my knees. I graduated on my momma's birthday; "Thank You, Jesus" is all I have to say. My Teacher Mrs. Alexander had much love, sent from heaven up above. I passed the exit exam and to her R.I.P., thank you, ma'am. Today I'm a woman all grown up & stuff, getting here sure been rough. I have even faced death a time or two but my God has always brought me through. Now I'm married and we are one twain sometimes I feel like I'm losing my mind. All his cheating, lies, naming calling, we stay brawling. I have fallen deep, now I'm seeking GOD for my peace. No matter what I am going to hold on and stay strong, but I feel so alone. I've been talked about and cursed out; people hate me who don't know the first thing about me. I've been lied to, used and abused, but JESUS's name to me is good news. I guess you are tired of hearing about my life. Please believe it's nothing nice—I'm nobody that you can see. GOD can save us from a life of misery. That's why I say "DON'T" PITY ME.

By Jacqueline Thomas

TIME WILL TELL

04-01-20

Where we are going is all up to us. Slow down, why are you in a rush? Stop and take a look around. When you are in trouble there is no one to be found, but the man up above who showers us with love. What we do, most of us, what we want is continuing in our sins. It wouldn't hurt to pray every now and then. We didn't wake ourselves up this morning. We need to get the Bible out and start learning about our Creator, the one who made us. Jesus died to save our souls. We need to get in line and make heaven our goal, 'cause there are so many things we are not being told. Satan is out to seek and destroy; he wants us to go to hell. GOD wants us to save ourselves. The choice is up to you. God is not going to make you. He gave us freedom to do what we want down here on earth. If we continue in sin, we will end up in the dirt, to wake up in a time full of destruction with fire. Please believe me: GOD is no liar.

Sinners will receive their reward which is HELL. If we live right we will get to go to heaven. To some people that ain't nothing. They just don't know what they will be missing—streets made of gold, a mansion, no need for cash, no need to look sad. That is a happy place where all our troubles will be wiped away and we will get to see JESUS's face. I don't wish that no one goes to hell; that's why I say TIME WILL TELL.

By Jacqueline Thomas

HE HAS ALWAYS BEEN THERE

4-01-20

Sometimes I wonder, am I really loved? And then I think about Jesus, and all my wonders and my fears just disappear. I know I am a sinner, that I don't deny. That's why I try, try, try to get myself together and learn how to love my sistas & my brothers. The devil is always busy trying to make a big scene. That's why my mind and my heart need to be cleaned. I am always getting into something but He is there to bail me out—all I have to do is SHOUT or call upon His name. Then things will change, in the blink of an eye or a touch of His hand. I personally know JESUS is the man. Trials and tribulations are always at my feet but I do know JESUS is in my reach. None of us is perfect and we will never be. I am trying to get closer to Jesus. Please don't hinder me. Every night in my prayers I thank GOD, 'cause HE HAS ALWAYS BEEN THERE.

By Jacqueline Thomas

DON'T COMPLAIN

04-01-20

When you are broke and don't have a dime, smile—everything is fine. The LORD is working and He will be right on time. Call Him; there is power in His name.
   Don't complain.

   When rent and bills are due and there is no one to help you, stay strong; trouble don't last long. He is still the same.
   Don't complain.

   When you come across a problem and you don't know what to do. Pray and let Jesus guide you. He will see you through. He don't change.
   Don't complain.

When you feel used and abused, nine times out of ten you feel like a fool. Keep your head up and press on. You're in the right lane.
Don't complain.

Through trials and tribulations, when you're in a bad situation, it's time to hit the knee way station. Face God to tell Him about your trouble. He will answer 'cause He loves us regardless. You can stand the rain.
Don't complain.

When you don't have a car to get around (maybe because it's broke down), and there is no one to be found to give you a ride, swallow your pride. Things will change.
Don't complain.

When you lose a loved one, family member, lover, or friend, and you feel like you're lost, Jesus has a shoulder to lend. He won't put more on you than you can bear. Remember, He is the one who answers prayer. That's another one of those things.
Don't complain.

When the world began He gave us His word. GOD is the word; He created heaven and earth, we were created from dust not dirt. I know we can stand a little hurt, it only makes us stronger. When we die, the pain we'll have no longer; we don't have to suffer, our loved ones will remain.
DON'T COMPLAIN.

By Jacqueline Thomas

"MY GOD"

4-1-20

*Y*ou have always been here from the start. God, You are the one who created my heart. You pick me up when I'm down, you turn my frown into a smile. You always let me know I'm Your child.

You bless me. You let the devil test me, and by my side You'll always be; You never leave. You are my rock and my shield, and all my wounds You heal.

God, I can always tell You how I feel. God, I know You are real. When nobody else knows the deal, You already know, and Your love continues to flow as well as show; in God I want to grow.

I know You are always close to let me know You care and no burdens I have to bear. It makes me feel good, as well as smart, to say, I thank You for being MY GOD!

By Jacqueline Thomas

"A FRIEND INDEED"

4-1-20

On You I always call, on my knees I always crawl, to ask you LORD for your love & protection & to forgive me for my transgressions LORD I'm glad I met ya.

GOD, I need You here on earth while I'm experiencing so much hurt. LORD I'll need You, even when I'm put in the dirt. Jesus, I thank GOD for His birth. Jesus's blood paid the price, the ultimate sacrifice to save our lives. Lord, I dreed when I see your eyes. Lord you are my everything, my rock and my shield, my provider; oh, how I love You Jehovah Jireh, the Alpha, the Omega, the beginning and the end. I call on you every day, not just every now and then. LORD, I thank You for being my friend and always having a shoulder to lend. I don't have to beg and plead, You said ask and believe and we will receive, that's why You are "A FRIEND INDEED!"

By Jacqueline Thomas

"PRAY"

4-1-20

Thank GOD for waking you up this morning enclosed in your right mind. Nowadays the blind lead the blind. Thank GOD at all times in and out of season, everything happens for a reason. GOD is the one we need to be pleasing. The LORD deserves ALL the praise, you know we are living in our last days, from the cradle to the grave. Brothers killing brothers, daughters hating their mothers. Children killing their parents. There is so much happening. Babies having babies, fornicating, adultery, disease—it's time to get on our knees. Some people just won't believe. Hurricanes, tornadoes, storms, LORD I know we are being warned. The old people used to say "he's coming like a thief in the night." People, we have to get right. Some things we go through are meant, some things we can prevent; some people are heaven sent. The LORD is an ALL seeing and knowing

GOD I'm gonna make you proud of me

GOD; for Him there is nothing too hard. We need to stay near GOD to keep the evil away, so PRAY.

By Jacqueline Thomas

"NEVER ALONE"

4-1-20

*G*OD, You are always here; You never leave my side. LORD, when I go to church I can feel you way down on the inside. It starts at my head and ends at my feet. LORD, thank You for never leaving me. No one will ever take Your place. The things You've done for me will never be erased. I keep them in my head. GOD, Your fury is what I dread; have mercy on us, LORD, for we know not what we do. My mission is to find You. I always tell them the truth. I say You're not gone; repent and everything we do comes right back, I know. Dig one ditch you gotta dig two. That other ditch is for you. I tell them to turn the other cheek; that's what the Bible tells me. I just call You from my heart—it's a phone. It makes me feel good to know I'm NEVER ALONE.

By Jacqueline Thomas

LIFT MY HEAD UP!

4-1-20

Most of the time I feel like crying. Sometimes I feel like dying. Jesus, You cross my mind then I'm fine. I think I will keep trying. Nothing that I have to go through can ever make me question You. Happy is what You want me to be. I will be. GOD, I know You are REAL. LORD, You know the deal and how I feel. Satan's out to steal my joy. GOD, you are the real McCoy, the Alpha and the Omega the beginning & the end. I know you will be there through thick and thin. I'm turning my back on sin; with You by my side I'll win. I lean on You all the time. GOD You are always on my mind. I love to give You praise for making ways. When I seem to get stuck all I do is LIFT MY HEAD UP.

By Jacqueline Thomas

MY BLESSINGS

4-1-20

*E*ver since I was a young lady, thinking about when you would come it drove me crazy. I'm a woman now and I want you even more. I failed but I want you to score. I want to shower you with love and affection and I will always be your protection. In you I will find true love; I will know definitely you're from above. I think about you all the time. I fantasize on how labor will be and the day you come to me. I will be a mommy, even your best friend. I'll try to keep you from making the mistakes I made back then. When I was a child my momma gave me an inch and I took a mile. You will make me smile and press on, 'cause sometimes I'm not strong. 'Nobody loves me' is how I feel. I know you will. I'm begging for to you to come into my life. Alright, I will wait. Until that day when my cake been baked. I can't wait to see your face. Right now I'm stressing, sitting waiting on "MY BLESSINGS."

By Jacqueline Thomas

"GLITTER & GOLD"

4-1-20

As a baby you know I had to crawl before I walked. Everything was just a thought. I couldn't speak so everything and everybody was new to me. I didn't know that was the best time in my life for me. Then I didn't know about misery. I had life without sin, laughing, I was a baby then. They say babies see angels, the ones who protect us from danger. During that time, everybody was strangers. As kids growing up we all complained. Then things we couldn't change. Eighteen years in our parents' house we remained. Now we're grown, time to experience life on our own. We go through a little heartache and pain; back then we figured "No pain, no gain." Paying bills, being ill—stressed, depressed, and all the rest.

Trials tribulations those are some of the things we facing. No problems, burdens, heartache, pain are too big for JESUS. POWER in His name, victory is what I claim, so some things we must change. There are only two roads to take. We have to start now, before it's too late. The devil can't have my soul. GOD didn't say it will be "GLITTER & GOLD."

By Jacqueline Thomas

"JESUS"

4-1-20

J is for JUST the type of person You are, my shining star

E is for ETERNAL life, what You promised we will receive if we live right & believe.

S is for SPECIAL, 'cause that's what You are, GOD's only begotten SON

U is for UNIQUE, 'cause another person like You will never be.

S is for SWEET, 'cause You multiplied the fish so thousands could eat!

"GOD"

4-1-20

G is for GIVING, 'cause You gave Your SON willingly

O is for ONE, 'cause You're the only GOD in my heart

D is for DOVE, which is a sign from up above that reminds us of Your love.

"FORGIVE ME"

4-1-20

I always act like I got something to do. I know I need to get the Bible out and learn more about You. I already know what You can do. You always pull me through. I need to get my priorities together and stay true; one minute I'm up and the next I'm down, there is no one around. But You, LORD, I pray You stay. Don't give me up to a reprobate mind—You deserve all my time. Don't leave me PLEASE, where will I go? That's why my love I have to show. People will know I am a BLESSED child. I know I'll be here a little while. I smile sometimes when I really want to cry. LORD, You wipe the tears from my eyes. LORD, You never promised the road would be easy. But You said You wouldn't leave me. Satan can't have my soul, to You I belong. I wanna walk the streets of gold live, forever in a mansion heaven. Oh, what a BLESSING! I will never be sick anymore or be without. When I think of it, it makes me wanna

SHOUT. People talked about You and did you wrong. LORD, I thank You for being strong. LORD You paid the price for our lives. GOD, I know You're coming back one day or one night. The time, no one knows; I just hope my eyes won't be closed. I want to see. LORD, PLEASE "FORGIVE ME."

By Jacqueline Thomas

"SMILE"

4-1-20

A frown is something people do not want to see, especially folks like you and me.

A smile will go the extra mile to lift someone up. They may be down, feeling sick, stressed, depressed, or in some mess. I don't know the rest. Anything could be on their mind. They would say they're fine knowing all the time they lying.

A smile from you or me just may be the key to lifting their spirit. Giving advice, sometimes people don't wanna hear it. So give them a great big smile and let GOD handle the rest. He knows what's best. Life, it's just a test. So smile for me—smiling is a sign of being at PEACE. Now, let me see them teeth.

Grin, for you are GOD's child, and for that you should ALWAYS "SMILE."

By Jacqueline Thomas

"KEEP STRIVING"

4-1-20

Through this life, life may throw you a couple of curveballs. GOD is on your side; you can stand tall through it ALL. Stand strong—trouble don't last long, before you know it it's gone, so don't tarry along. Hold your head high up to the sky. GOD has all POWER, so He is in control. The devil's mad 'cause he can't have your soul. Stand bold. Keep trying to make it to the streets of gold. In Heaven, where evil has no place, we will be with GOD every day. Everything is going to be okay. Continue to pray and read your BIBLE, learn of JESUS's disciples, let GOD guide you where He wants you to be; the rest is HISTORY. GOD has perfect timing, so sistas and brothers, "KEEP STRIVING."

GOD, COME IN

4-1-20

Praying, I have so much to be thankful for. The roof over my head, food to eat, good health; those things just can't be beat. I have eyes to see, legs to walk, and mouth to talk. Priceless; those things can't be bought. I'm in the right frame of mind. I have all my limbs and I'm able to use them. Praying, thank You LORD for being a friend. I can call on you anytime, not just every now and then. I'm trying to walk right with all my might. I want to gain eternal life. This world is so corrupt. Lord, I know You're like a volcano ready to erupt. Jesus, please save my soul, and while I walk my hand please hold. I wanna walk the streets of GOLD. No more pain, hurt, or sorrow; no need to worry about tomorrow. No need for money—a dollar I won't have to borrow. No more evil or deceit, 'cause Satan You have beat.

Lord, You got the key to hell, so we're free. The Alpha and Omega, the beginning and the ending. The truth and the light. LORD, you are out of sight, dynamite. Praying, I hope I'm ready when You come like a thief in the night. I can't wait for that day when all darkness is put away. Thank You, GOD, for preparing a better place. LORD, we won when You gave Your ONLY BEGOTTEN son. Praying who knock praying on. Don't stop, the clock is ticking. Listening—do I hear a horn? I'm running to look at the sky. I'm trembling. I'm scared; know why, there is FIRE in His eyes. Oh, it's about to storm; false alarm. Jesus, guide my footsteps through this life and then I know I'll win. Hey, GOD, COME IN.

By Jacqueline Thomas

GOD, COME IN

4-1-20

Praying, I have so much to be thankful for. The roof over my head, food to eat, good health; those things just can't be beat. I have eyes to see, legs to walk, and mouth to talk. Priceless; those things can't be bought. I'm in the right frame of mind. I have all my limbs and I'm able to use them. Praying, thank You LORD for being a friend. I can call on you anytime, not just every now and then. I'm trying to walk right with all my might. I want to gain eternal life. This world is so corrupt. Lord, I know You're like a volcano ready to erupt. Jesus, please save my soul, and while I walk my hand please hold. I wanna walk the streets of GOLD. No more pain, hurt, or sorrow; no need to worry about tomorrow. No need for money—a dollar I won't have to borrow. No more evil or deceit, 'cause Satan You have beat.

Lord, You got the key to hell, so we're free. The Alpha and Omega, the beginning and the ending. The truth and the light. LORD, you are out of sight, dynamite. Praying, I hope I'm ready when You come like a thief in the night. I can't wait for that day when all darkness is put away. Thank You, GOD, for preparing a better place. LORD, we won when You gave Your ONLY BEGOTTEN son. Praying who knock praying on. Don't stop, the clock is ticking. Listening—do I hear a horn? I'm running to look at the sky. I'm trembling. I'm scared; know why, there is FIRE in His eyes. Oh, it's about to storm; false alarm. Jesus, guide my footsteps through this life and then I know I'll win. Hey, GOD, COME IN.

By Jacqueline Thomas

"IT HAPPENED"

4-1-20

I met you as a little girl in elementary. I didn't know I would see you a century later. I guess that's one of GOD's favors. We use to kid around and crack jokes. We knew all the time, we wanted to get close. One day at work we kissed. Playing around with you, one thing I did miss. Back then we didn't see each other that much. Then I saw you in the clubhouse, I had to stay in touch. Adultery is something I said I wouldn't do. I lied, because I ran across you. What's next? I really don't know. Let's just let it flow. Let's take our time, relax, and unwind. If I said I didn't love you I would be lying. I never thought you'd be mine after all this time. If only for one night, but we just can't seem to get it right. With Jesus in our life, we can do anything. I asked for a friendship, not a ring. You said you would be there for me. Often, I feel lonely. Constantly on my mind. You make me happy instead of crying. GOD works in mysterious ways. I will never forget that day. That's all I have to say. Sinner, repent. I don't know, maybe it was meant. I will never be the same, I know my family's clapping. I'm so glad it HAPPENED!

I LOVE YOU

4-1-20

I love you. Do you love me? Why don't you love me? 'Cause you feel that I'm nobody. Maybe because you don't know me. Do you think I'm beneath you? That's so not true. Oh, because you got money. Well let me tell you something, honey. You are so funny. Money is the root of all evil. The love of money has taken control of many people. They will sell their souls for a dollar. They feel UNSTOPPABLE. Money can't save their life, it has no price. Some people kill, steal, and tell lies. Don't let money take your pride. Please open your eyes. STAY true; don't let money control anything you do. Happiness can't be bought. It's temporary. The reason I'm telling you it's necessary. GOD is our main concern, oh yes, you will learn. Our goal in life is to live right. One day we will get to see his face. We will live forever. We don't have to go to hell, unlike the devil. GOD loves us more than we love ourselves. The wages of sin is death. I'm just speaking the truth. Only because I LOVE YOU.

Jacqueline Thomas

"LIFE"

4-1-20

None of us asked to come here. Do I make myself clear? Listen let me get in your ear. GOD saw fit so our births were meant. We all have a purpose in life. All we've got to do is what's right. One day we'll see the light. Love the people who are in your life; everybody you know and don't know. GOD is love, so let your love show. In Jesus we have to grow.

    We all have problems, He can solve them. Trials and tribulation. He can pull you through any situation. Hurt and pain. God don't change. There is POWER in His name. If we go to hell, we will be to blame. Victory is what I claim. JESUS died for all of your sins way back then. So we win. Yes, we won. GOD gave His only begotten son. Jesus died on that rugged cross. We all were lost. Please turn away from sin. Yes, JESUS paid the price to save our LIFE.

By Jacqueline Thomas

"TIME"

4-1-20

Tomorrow is not promised. We got to start today. If we start with ourselves we can make the world a better place. Every day, we go on in our lives like we don't have any concerns. We will learn. Living in this life, we've got to treat people right, no matter what color or race they are. That in itself will take us far. Stop the hating and faking; too many lives have been taken. We have to come together for the next generation. We are all sisters and brothers. So stop downing each other. One day we will see GOD's face. He is coming back, and not to play. Like a thief in the night, can you imagine the sight? Everything is going to have life. So we got to get right. Too many people dying, mommas crying. People sick; some have cancer or disease. We need to stay on our knees. Asking GOD to please help us. Enough is enough. This little light of mine, I'm gonna let shine. I hope it's right on TIME.

"PRAISE"

4-1-20

Why are you stressing? GOD can work it out NO DOUBT. Never put your faith in man/woman; they will let go of your hand.

Maybe that's a part of GOD's plans to build you up, so you can stand on your own. Life will make you strong. Remember to whom you belong

Relax, GOD's got you. He'll see you through. Ain't nothing GOD can't do. He will bind up your broken heart, turn you around and give you a brand-new start.

Straight to the church we need to march, to tell Him all about our trouble and how we feel. Our wounds He will heal. GOD is real. Chill, no burdens we have to bear. Just leave them there. Please don't worry, that's not the end of the story. Give Him the GLORY for making a way. Give GOD the PRAISE.

HELL ON EARTH

4-1-20

From the beginning of time, Jesus was our savior, the one who made us. Bone of His bone, flesh of His flesh. Life is a test. Don't cry for your family and friends who lay to rest. In this life we have a choice to make. JESUS is real, the devil is fake. Ups and downs, trials, tribulations, pain, rain, sickness, and death are some things we have to go through. Those are what make you. He never said it would be easy. He came and died for you and me. Nobody we know would have done that. We have a chance to live forever. The devil is clever. He wants us to take our minds off GOD and be entangled in this world. Our flesh, it's a mess. We have to be ready at all times. Please don't stay blind. Put Heaven on your mind. Don't listen to the devil; he is fake. There are only two roads to take. Get right before it's too late. We are all GOD's children—better yet, His kids. Don't let the devil get in you like he did the pig. Live life to the fullest or the best you know how. When it comes to heaven have no doubt. GOD is coming back to get us whether we are living or in the dirt, cause here to me is "HELL ON EARTH."

"NEVER LET ME DOWN"

4-1-20

Whatever I go through, LORD, I can always count on you. When my light gets dim. My chances seem slim. When I feel like all hope is gone. LORD You come along and lift my spirit. LORD I know You're near. I can feel it. I don't have to bear my cross alone. Sometimes I have to sing that song. I have been through the storm and the rain. I look back and see how far I have come. Even when I walked away, by my side You still stay. I get out of line. You put me back in place. There is so much going on here on earth. There is so much hurt, lies, deception, robbing, stealing, killing. To help someone, people are not willing. I am tired of all these devils and demons. They do evil things for no reason. Nowadays you can't tell the changes in the season. Everything Your Word speaks in the BIBLE, is at hand. Some things I can't understand. So I will smile instead of frown. LORD, YOU NEVER LET ME DOWN.

Jacqueline Thomas

"STOP THE VIOLENCE"

4-1-20

There is so much going on in the world today. We need to take time out and pray. Ask GOD to make a way for our kids. They are not safe. They can't even go outside and play. What happened to the good old days? We played hide and seek. When one parent cooked, all the kids could eat. Kick and volleyball we played in the middle of the street. We didn't have a Slip n' Slide. We would make one with a tarp and dishwashing liquid. Yes, it made a lot of bubbles if we used too much. We got in trouble. Simon Says and hop-scotch; we didn't have to worry that somebody'd shoot up the block. That was a time when people valued life. Mothers were moms and fathers were dads; now the women are trying to raise a family on their own, and that's sad. When momma spoke, you listened and paid attention to what she said. Kids are being misled. The kids are our next generation. We have no time to be wasting. Talk to the young boys. Tell them about guns, the difference between the real ones and the toys. Teach our young ladies how to be a lady. Education before the babies. What happened to the love? So many lives have been taken with a weapon. We sit back and do nothing. I couldn't sit back and keep the silence; let's PLEASE STOP THE VIOLENCE.

By Jacqueline Thomas

TELLING LIES

4-1-20

Some people will look you eye to eye. They know all the time they're telling a lie.
Sometimes the lies will be voluntary, when it wasn't even necessary.

    Tell the truth, what's wrong with you? Why lie? You got to tell three or more. I'm still not convinced. Telling a lie makes no sense. They say people would rather hear a lie. They don't wanna hear the truth; wait a minute. Sometimes they really do. That's still ain't right. GOD said a liar can't tarry in His sight. Remember, He's coming back like a thief in the night, so lies don't tell. Do you wanna go to hell? Telling the truth is simple. With lies you've got to remember what you said. Telling lies makes your own bed of corruptions and consequences. Telling a lie to me is senseless. So, take the honest route. The truth will come out. A liar GOD despises, so please quit TELLING LIES.

By Jacqueline Thomas

MERCY & GRACE

4-1-20

We get out of character. When we do, it sometimes causes laughter. We realize it's a part of a chapter in our life. If certain things we didn't go through, LORD, we wouldn't need You. We can look back and see where and who we used to be. The things we used to do we don't do anymore. That is what you call GROWTH.

    Where You are taking us to I don't know, but I gotta trust You. I know You care and You don't put any more on us than we can bear. You are all seeing &and knowing; Your love keeps us going. At times we feel faint. We know there is no such thing as can't. GOD, with You ALL things are possible. LORD with You guiding our footsteps, we can do the impossible. Really nothing even matters, 'cause You fight our battles. Whether they are big or small. LORD, You handle them all. On Your name I always call. You work it out. No doubt. Hallelujah in the highest praised, LORD with

GOD I'm gonna make you proud of me

You I'm so amazed. Please change our direction 'cause we need Your protection. Take us to a better space. We will keep the faith. Thanks for Your "MERCY & GRACE."

By Jacqueline Thomas

"RAIN"

4-1-20

LORD, I wonder. When it rains, are You crying? I heard people say that, are they lying? I know we cry. We cry when someone dies. When our hearts have been broken. Sometimes we cry tears of happiness. LORD, when You wipe away our sadness. The rain replenishes the dirt so the things from the earth can grow. The grass, trees, plants, fruits, and the vegetables. Without the rain, things would surely die and be dry. It would be like a desert not fit for habitation. It would eliminate our population. That's a bad situation to be facing. We need the rain. That's one thing I'm trying to make clear. Hey, lend me your ear. The water we drink comes from rain, just think. The water we use to bathe in. If we didn't have it, we would stink. Water flows in the river, lake, and the ocean. They all have different motions. LORD, I get the notion. If we didn't have some rain, certain things couldn't change. We all got to get on track. We got to be ready. LORD, I know You are coming back. The signs are here. The air is being attacked. That's a shame. LORD, please let it RAIN.

By Jaqueline Thomas

"LET GO"

4-1-20

Lonely is something I thought I would never be. On March 28, the day you married me, I was so happy during that time. I used to believe you were all mine. I found out that was not true. If I wasn't around, ain't no telling what you would do. I had trust, of course, it's a must. Things changed through the years. I got tired of wiping away my own tears. I guess that's why now I'm just sitting here. I'm clearing my mind, as well as my thoughts. Yasss, most of my sense has been bought. Plenty of lessons you have taught. Now we are not together, that's all your fault. I miss you. I miss you even more during the holidays. You just wouldn't change your ways. There was a time when you were my husband and I was your wife.

Back then you were my life. Even though you didn't do everything right. We used to fuss sometimes. We would fight. You started hanging in them streets. I guess you forgot about me. That is no place for a husband to be. Tempted by women. You started having those lust-filled feelings. During that time I wasn't dealing. I guess you went to them for sex and they were willing. One time you stayed out all night. My tongue I continued to bite. You started doing drugs. You made a big mistake. OK, how much was I supposed to take? I still tried to make it work. I felt like it was me you were out to hurt. Disrespect, no, I'm not with that. Putting your hands on me. Please, I will have your family looking awfully. It's too much. SO I LET GO.

By Jacqueline Thomas

"TO WHOM I BELONG"

4-1-20

This place is not my home. Like that saying goes, one day you're here and the next you're gone. Ever since I came into this world I've been done wrong. From so-called friends to my family. They smile in my face and, for no reason, they can't stand me. I can expect that from my enemies. Their hate I do see. Nowadays the new REAL is fake. I can't stand a snake. I will tell them to their face disloyalty. I will catch a case. So now I ride solo dolo. These people are cutthroat. That I already know. Slow down, Tedo, take a pause. Don't hate my swag. I be feeling like I'm bad. Yeah, go ahead and laugh; I'm just mad because of the jealousy. That's sad.

Some of us live one day at a time. Some of us were made to shine. Some of us drink liquor and not wine. I don't care what nobody else do. I'm handling mine. I don't have much. Whatever I got, I'm thankful. I'm thankful and that's enough. I keep pushing on 'cause I know TO WHOM I BELONG.

By Jacqueline Thomas

"SOME OF THEM"

4-1-20

*P*eople...
　　Some of them have gifts. When you come around your spirit lifts.

　　Some of them come around to help or encourage you. Some of them wanna stop what you're trying to do.

　　Some of them only for a season. Some of them came in your life for a reason. To teach you a lesson. Now they gone count your BLESSINGS!

　　Some of them you wish you never met. Some of them will leave you full of regret.

　　Some of them will have you screaming, "Who's next?"

　　Some of them came into your life to cause you pains.

　　Some of them will never change.

　　Some of them don't have a heart. Some of them you got to give to GOD!

　　Some of them like to pray.

Some of them wanna do things their way.

Some of them you can trust. To some of them you are not enough.

Some of them want to grow; some of them play slow, acting like they don't know.

Some of them wanna do right. Some of them make GOD the head of their life.

Some of them feel stuck.

Some of them fell down and never tried to get up.

Some of them, all they wanna do is ball.

Some of them are a lost cause. Some of them wanna change for their boys and girls.

Some of them live in their own world.

Some of them don't know there ain't but two roads you can take.

Some of them can't tell the real from the fake.

Some of them are all about a show. Some of them like being broke. Some of them will

Be there when you hurt.

Some of them come across as a jerk.

Some of them will have an impact. Some of them got what you lack and they got your

Back. Some of them are all about talk. Some of them know GOD is the boss.

Some of them are being deceived. Some of them get down on their knees to GOD AND

PLEAD.

Some of them don't even care. Some of them don't know NO burdens they have to bear.

"Some of Them"

Some of them are gonna make me take it there.

Sinners entering heaven is slim. I don't wanna be a "SOME OF THEM."

By Jacqueline Thomas

"GIVE ME A TOPIC"

4-1-20

I can write about anything. Rappers, they focus on the jewelry and the rings. Once upon a time I wanted to rap. I got hit by a car and that was a mishap. I really started to focus on my life. I've never ever really done right. The LORD has always been there protecting me. There is a lot I've learned and a lot I've got to see. I know I can be all that I want to be and I don't have to join the army. America is the land of the free and the home of the brave. Answer this question: what's going on in the world today? If you ask me, we all need to pray. It's like our NATION has been cursed. There is too much going on and too much hurt. I will be the first to speak. Right now we just need peace. Bring our soldiers home from the Middle East. We all need to come back together, one nation under GOD. I for one LOVE THE LORD. He created all our hearts. With this ink pen I write how I'm feeling, what he puts on my mind at that

time. So you know I can freestyle, but I'm God's child. He blessed my hands. For Him I stand. If you're reading this, it was in His plans, and we are safe 'cause we're in His hands! So I guess I will stop it. Do you want me to write?
GIVE ME A TOPIC.

By Jacqueline Thomas

"FASTING"

4-1-20

Fasting is good for your spirit; when GOD speaks, you can hear it. Fasting draws GOD near. It helps you see things clear. Because things are not always as they appear.

In GOD's Word He says you can't live off food alone. Pray He helps you stay strong. During that time, we need to pray and seek GOD's face. He will lead your way. He said when you fast don't wear a frown on your face so people will know; you aren't supposed to let it show. You're praying for a breakthrough, or to let something go. During fasting you will be tempted. Just know all toxins in you are being emptied. A sign of purification of the mind, soul, and body. In this world today fasting need to become a hobby. Everybody got their different ways how to; I know prayer and water, no food. That's how I was taught to do. It's like you making a sacrifice for GOD to change something sinful your life. GOD does answer prayer. All you have to do is leave it there. Don't waiver because you gave it to your Savior. The answer to all your questions GOD has. Seek and you shall find. We are His children . He doesn't want us blind. He is a spirit and He is the truth. He created me and you. We need Him to direct our path—all of us, so we won't do the things in our past. In this world right now and what's happening, we all need to come together and start FASTING.

BY Jaqueline Thomas

"CHANGE"

4-1-20

We gotta try to change. But we have to do it for ourselves. We all know the wages of sin is death. Stop downing each other and look at yourself. It starts there. When we have run out, JESUS is all we got left. There is no doubt about it. His name, I love to shout it. If He is not, you need to make Him the HEAD of your life. Then things will turn out right. We can't make it in this life on our own. The way we should live has been shown. When Jesus came down here on earth, He also experienced the hurt. He still was His father's mission. A lot Jesus went through the Bible didn't mention. He endured a lot for you and me. He died on Calvary. He told the Father, "Forgive them, for they know not what they do." He was telling the truth. Killing our Savior, that was major. Without a cause. Sometimes in our life we need to take a pause and give thanks to the LORD our GOD for all that He has done. He gave His only begotten son. We can't go on doing the same things. We all must make a CHANGE.

By Jacqueline Thomas

"CAN'T JUDGE ME"

4-1-20

So you're talking, got my name in your mouth. What's all this fuss about? Hatin' 'cause I got gold in my mouth. Wait, let me find out. Maybe that's some he-say, she-say and they say. I'm not gonna let them ruin my day. Maybe they like my style. It could be my swag 'cause I'm always smiling; it must make 'em mad. I'm not Michael Jackson, I ain't bad. They just don't know what I have been through; most of them don't have a clue. I found a love that is true. I got a new mindset. Nope, GOD's not done with me yet. Those things I will never forget. They didn't kill me. I had to learn to let go of my insecurities and people that no longer served a purpose to be in my life. I'm just trying to get it right. I have done some things that I'm not proud of. Those things came from reacting to love. One sin isn't worse than the other. That's the problem. You should have been taught to love you sistas & brothers. No matter what we come across in life, things could be worse. It's ok to get a little dirt on your shirt. Nothing belongs to us on earth. What's inside me people don't see. I don't have time for drama no more. I want peace. I only have one life to live. I'm just keeping it real. The truth don't need a sugar coat. About the LORD I brag and boast. Jesus is all that and some more. He died on that cross for all our sins back then. So you see, you CAN'T JUDGE ME.

By Jacqueline Thomas

"FAVOR AIN'T FAIR"

4-1-20

For as long as I can remember, I've been giving the LORD praise. Yes, I have seen Him make ways. I have seen Him open and close doors. God has reached way down and picked me off the floor. At one time I was on my dying bed. GOD turned it around instead I woke up out of a coma. I had been in for three weeks. My auntie came in the room. GOD let me speak. I had head trauma. I got hit by a vehicle and knocked forty feet. I landed in the middle of the street. I know it was GOD who saved me. I flipped six times in midair. I landed on my face. Looking at me today, you don't even see a trace. You can't imagine what I've been through. GOD is who I look to and the hills from which come my help. I know I didn't make it this far by myself. When I talk about GOD, I'm speaking because we have a personal relationship. People don't wanna hear it and that's a trip. GOD is no respecter of persons. He loves us all. He blesses us whether it's big or small. We all have different wants and needs. It's GOD I'm trying to please. He's been in my life since I was young. I learned from my mom & grandmom that Jesus is the one. They told me because they care. One thing I do know: "FAVOR AIN'T FAIR."

By Jacqueline Thomas

"CORONAVIRUS"

4-1-20

You came at a time when we least expected. You got relationships being neglected. People are walking around like we are all infected. Many lives you have taken. Corona, you are here so you ain't faking. A virus; I consider you a germ. On that term, more about you doctors are trying to learn. Our families at this time are everybody's concern. On the old generation you're really having an effect. Corona's spreading fast. I wonder who is next. You've got to be stopped. Too many people have died. Corona is affecting us nationwide. I mean, it's in every state. Everybody's making sure everything's sanitized. One thing you got to realize: from our fate you can't run and hide. God didn't give us a spirit of fear. Do I make myself clear? All we can do is pray the doctors find a cure one day. Thank GOD that everybody that got it, they haven't been taken away. You see some of the TV every day. The

Bible is fulfilling; people will see who JESUS is no matter if they are willing. Things such as this have been prophesized. My people, open up your eyes. I can see, don't stay blind. We are drawing closer to the end of time. GOD needs to be on our minds. Everything happens for a reason. Remember, things have a season. A change will come. Many of us heart that song. We can't go outside and paint the town. None of our friends and family can come around. Everything we touched got to be wiped down. Nobody's smiling, everybody's wearing a frown. Some of us can't go to work—that's gotta hurt. We have to make a living; bills keeping coming. So, we got to keep giving. It's really bad; we can't even go to church. GOD is married to the church, so you know He's hurt. But He dwells within. My advice is turn away from sin. This is deep. We have to stay six feet apart. For some of us, that's really hard. I'm used to giving kisses and hugs and showing some form of love. Especially when I come across someone I haven't seen in a minute. I'm sick of this epidemic. No more than twenty-five now ten in a room. We got to get a handle on this soon. When I go out to eat, I can't sit down in the restaurant seat. When I go to the grocery store or pay a bill, everybody's walking around like they're ill. At work someone is wiping and spraying behind me as if I'm nasty. This whole thing is taking a hold of me. Corona is affecting my sleep. I pray every day, so I know GOD is guiding my feet. He will take care of you and me. I try not to worry. I know this not the end of my story. To GOD be the glory. The LORD is the HEAD of my life. I know He is in control. So I stand bold, not on my tippy-toes. No games, no pool, no parties; the little ones are brokenhearted. Do you hear what I'm saying? No kids outside playing. No contact, and you know opposites attract. Relationships are being pushed back. Corona added up is the sum of 666 if you count the letters of the alphabet. GOD is the only one who can handle this. So pray while you are in your home. He promised never to leave us alone. He will take care of his people. Jesus said before sin enter heaven a camel can fit through a needle. His Word is true, and there is nothing He can't do. He is our Savior, the Creator, the Alpha and Omega. He still reigns. Remember power is in His name. To save our souls, Jesus came; of Him never be ashamed. Corona is here, that we can't change, but GOD can do anything we can't do anything about. GOD's got it, don't you doubt it. Leave it here in His hands. It may be hard to understand. Everything seems to work out in GOD's plans. GOD is the man. It's hard to keep the silence. We all have been affected in different ways by Coronavirus.

By Jacqueline Thomas

www.ingramcontent.com/pod-product-compliance
Ingram Content Group UK Ltd.
Pitfield, Milton Keynes, MK11 3LW, UK
UKHW022221230420
12048UKWH00016BA/978